Contents

Police Car

Police cars are used to reach the scene of a crime or accident quickly, to take people to the police station, or to patrol an area.

Mechanic Mike's Machines

Rescue Vehicles

Franklin Watts
This edition published in the UK in 2016 by The Watts Publishing Group

Copyright © 2014 David West Children's Books

Designed and illustrated by David West

Dewey number 629.2'25
PB ISBN: 978 1 4451 5182 3

Printed in Malaysia

Franklin Watts
An imprint of
Hachette Children's Group
Part of The Watts Publishing Group
Carmelite House
50 Victoria Embankment
London EC4Y 0DZ

An Hachette UK Company.
www.hachette.co.uk

www.franklinwatts.co.uk

MECHANIC MIKE'S MACHINES RESCUE VEHICLES
was produced for Franklin Watts by
David West Children's Books, 6 Princeton Court, 55 Felsham Road, London SW15 1AZ

Mechanic Mike says:
Mike will tell you
something more about
the machine.

Find out what type
of engine drives
the machine.

Discover
something you
didn't know.

Is it fast or slow?
Top speeds are
given here.

How many people
operate it?

Get your
amazing
fact here!

Some police forces use fast cars, such as Porsches, to follow speeding drivers.

 This is a Holden Monaro car. It can go from 0 to 160 kilometres per hour in 4.8 seconds.

 Police cars usually patrol with two officers inside.

 Did you know that police cars use flashing lights and sirens when there is an emergency?

 This car has a **supercharged** 5.7-litre petrol engine.

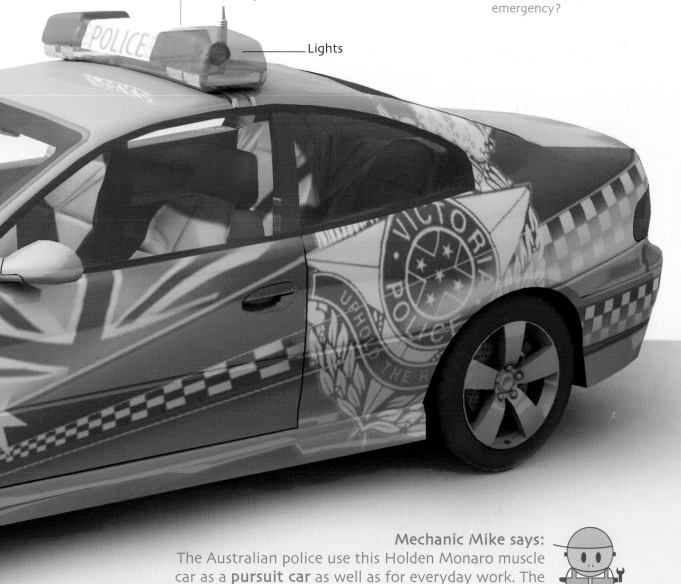

Lights

Mechanic Mike says:
The Australian police use this Holden Monaro muscle car as a **pursuit car** as well as for everyday work. The bright paintwork makes the car easy to see.

This Type III ambulance has a 6.8-litre petrol engine.

Did you know that ambulances pulled by horses were first used by the French army in 1793?

Ambulances usually have a crew of two. They are a driver with medical training and a **paramedic**.

Ambulances need to cruise at a speed of 105 kilometres per hour and have to be able to pass vehicles at 113 kilometres per hour.

The first motorised ambulance was used in Chicago in February, 1899.

Ambulance

Ambulances are used to rush to the scene of an emergency. They use flashing lights and sirens to warn people they are coming.

Mechanic Mike says:
Patients travel to hospital in the back of the ambulance. A paramedic uses special equipment to care for them.

Fire Engine

Fire engines don't just put out fires. They rescue people too. This turntable ladder fire engine can reach people trapped in high buildings.

Not all fire engines have ladders. Some carry water and hoses so they can spray water on to the fire.

Fire engines can go no faster than 121 kilometres per hour.

This fire engine has a crew of three firefighters.

Did you know a turntable ladder can extend to 30 metres? That means it can reach to the 13th floor of a building.

Fire engines are powered by **diesel engines**.

Telescopic ladder

Turntable

Mechanic Mike says:
This telescopic ladder is in sections that can slide out to the length needed.

Tow Truck

Emergency road services send out tow trucks to rescue cars and trucks that have broken down. If the vehicle cannot be repaired at the roadside, it will be towed to the nearest garage.

Mechanic Mike says:
Tow trucks are also called breakdown trucks or recovery trucks.

Most tow trucks have a winch to pull the vehicle on to the back of a **flatbed**.

 Although they have powerful engines, their maximum speed is 90 kilometres per hour.

 These trucks are usually operated by one person.

 Tow trucks use diesel engines as they have better pulling power than petrol engines. Trucks like this one have 12-litre engines.

 Did you know that massive tow trucks like this one can tow large, heavy vehicles like trucks and buses?

Winch

JACKSON'S TRUCK REPAIR

FRIENDLY SERVICE

11

This Honda motorbike has an 1084 cc petrol engine.

Did you know paramedic motorbikes have flashing lights and sirens just like police cars and ambulances?

A paramedic motorbike carries only one person.

This Honda ST1100 has a top speed of 215.6 kilometres per hour.

In Southern Sudan paramedic motorbikes have sidecars to carry pregnant women and injured people to a hospital.

Light

Siren

Mechanic Mike says:
Paramedic motorbikes are also known as motorbike ambulances.

12

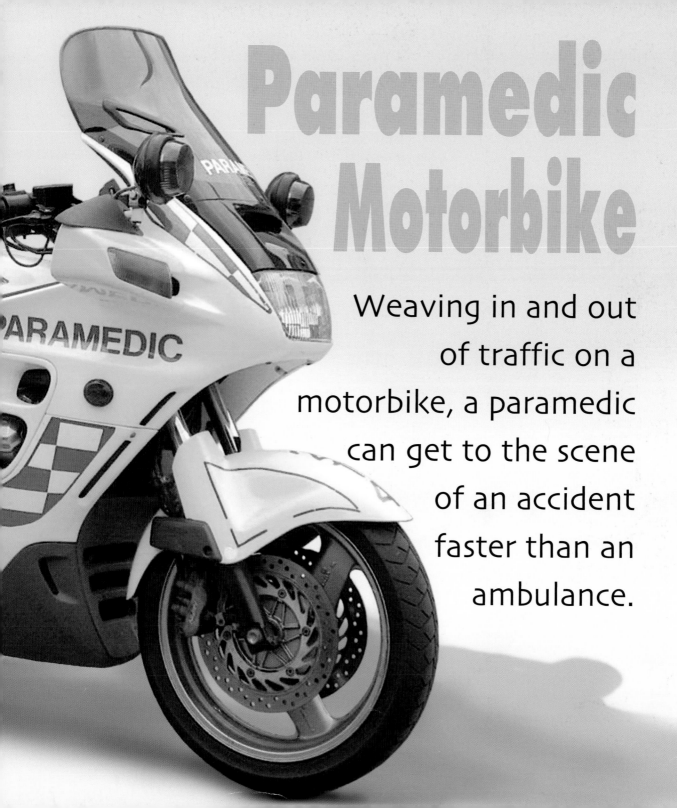

Paramedic Motorbike

Weaving in and out of traffic on a motorbike, a paramedic can get to the scene of an accident faster than an ambulance.

13

Air Ambulance

Sometimes a patient needs to get to hospital urgently. Air ambulance helicopters rescue people from motorway and city accidents and can reach hospitals much faster than other ambulances.

Mechanic Mike says:
Air ambulance helicopters are also used to reach people on mountains, at sea and in other areas of rough terrain or in locations far from other services.

Helicopters can take off and land vertically.

Did you know that ambulance helicopters were first used by the US army during the Korean War (1950–53)?

This helicopter can cruise at 226 kilometres per hour.

Air ambulances usually have a pilot and a one or two-person crew.

These helicopters use **turboshaft** engines to power the rotor blades.

G-DORS

AIR AMBULANCE SERVICE

Mountain Rescue

Mountain rescue teams use four-wheel drive vehicles such as Land Rovers to carry their equipment over rugged land.

Mechanic Mike says:
There are some places even helicopters cannot reach. Mountain rescue teams find the injured people and carry them on stretchers to a place where an air ambulance helicopter can land.

BRECON MOUNTAIN RESCUE

Vehicles like these use **turbo-charged** diesel engines.

Did you know that mountain rescue teams sometimes use dogs to help find injured climbers?

This vehicle can carry up to seven people plus equipment.

They have a top speed of about 161 kilometres per hour, but these vehicles are designed to travel at much lower speeds.

Vehicles with four-wheel drive (4x4) are able to travel over rough terrain as all four wheels are being powered by the engine.

17

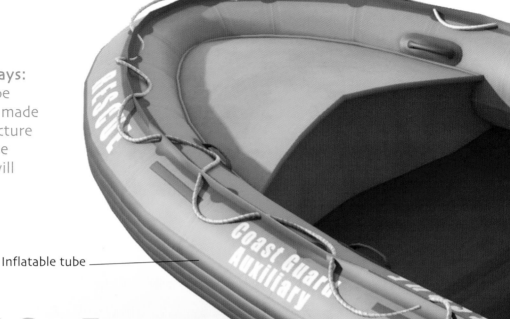

Inflatable tube ——

Lifeboat

People in trouble at sea, but close to shore are rescued by lifeboats like this RIB (Rigid Inflatable Boat). RIBs are easily steered around rocks and through shallow water and rough waves.

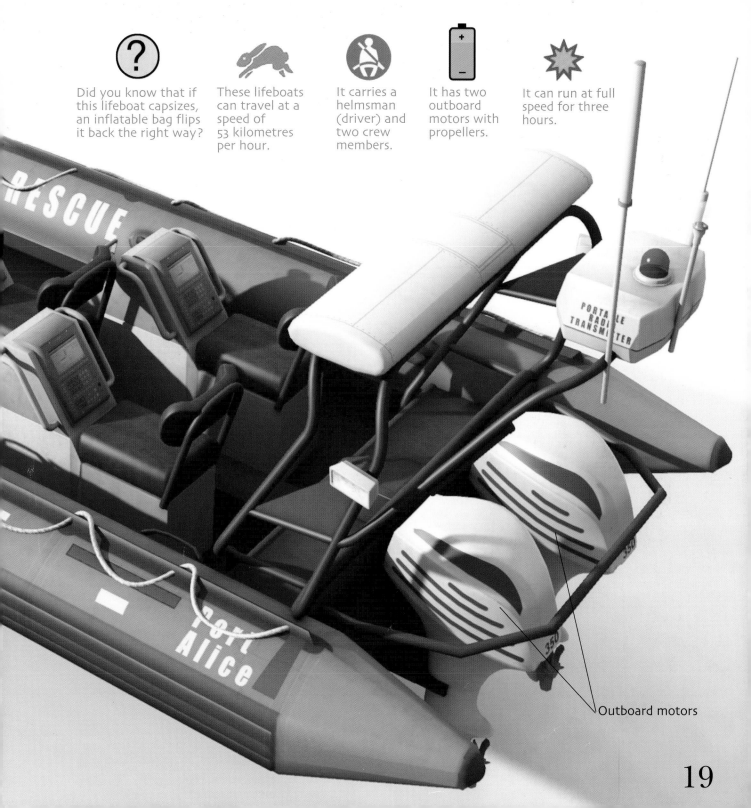

Did you know that if this lifeboat capsizes, an inflatable bag flips it back the right way?

These lifeboats can travel at a speed of 53 kilometres per hour.

It carries a helmsman (driver) and two crew members.

It has two outboard motors with propellers.

It can run at full speed for three hours.

PORTABLE RADIO TRANSMITTER

RESCUE

Port Alice

Outboard motors

This is the Sikorsky HH-60J. It has radar for searching that gives its nose an unusual shape.

Did you know that the hoist on the left hand side can lift people from 61 metres below?

The Sikorsky HH-60 Jayhawk can reach 333 kilometres per hour for short periods. It can fly at 259 kilometres per hour for six to seven hours.

This helicopter has a crew of four. It can hoist up to six additional people on board.

It has two turboshaft engines powering the rotor blades.

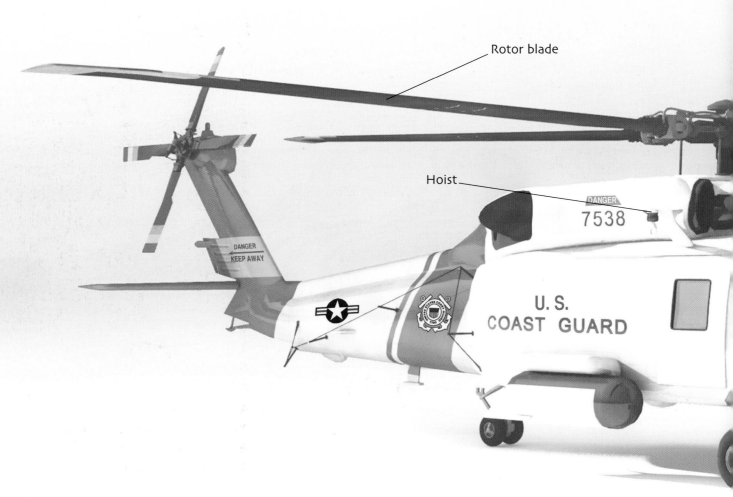

Rotor blade

Hoist

DANGER

7538

DANGER
KEEP AWAY

U.S.
COAST GUARD

Rescue Helicopter

Coastguard helicopters perform search and rescue around the coast, from rescuing people who have slipped off cliffs to saving crews from sinking ships.

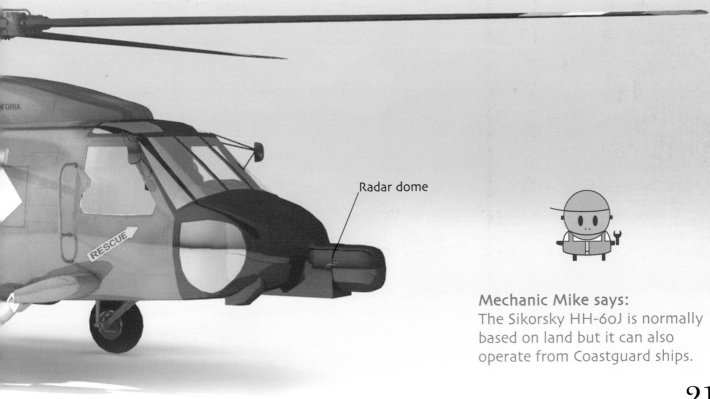

Radar dome

RESCUE

Mechanic Mike says:
The Sikorsky HH-60J is normally based on land but it can also operate from Coastguard ships.

Some countries' armed forces use large, modified airliners as flying hospitals to transfer patients over long distances.

 Did you know that the first air ambulances were modified **biplanes** during World War I?

 This Beechcraft Super King Air can cruise at 509 kilometres per hour.

 Usually there is one pilot and at least two medical crew members.

This plane has two **turboprop** engines.

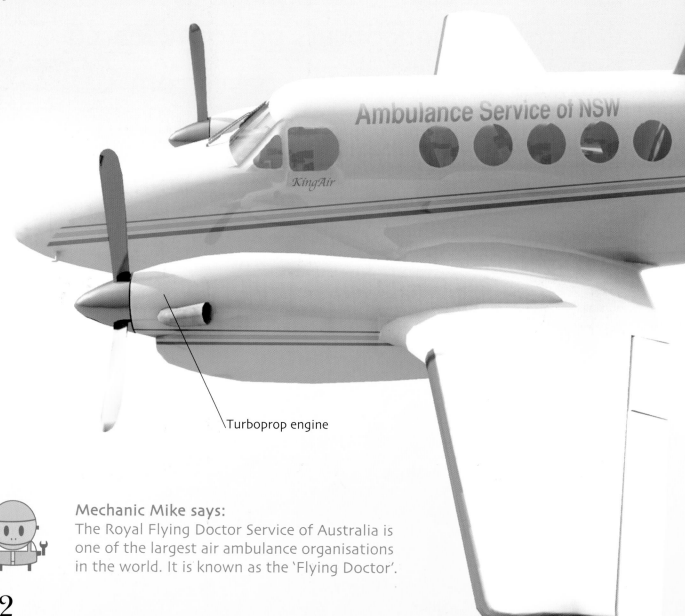

Turboprop engine

 Mechanic Mike says:
The Royal Flying Doctor Service of Australia is one of the largest air ambulance organisations in the world. It is known as the 'Flying Doctor'.

VH-MSH

Flying Doctor

As well as helicopters, light planes are also used as air ambulances. They are essential in places like Australia where there are people living in remote places.

Glossary

biplanes
Early planes with two sets of wings, one above the other.

diesel engines
Engines using diesel fuel.

flatbed
A flat rear part of a truck without sides or a roof.

inflatable
Filled with air.

paramedic
A person with medical training who works in emergency situations.

pursuit cars
Police cars that are fast enough for high speed chases and response calls.

supercharged
Extra power supplied to an engine by a supercharger.

turbo-charged
Extra power supplied to an engine by a turbine driven by exhaust gases.

turboprop
An engine similar to a jet that turns a propeller.

turboshaft
An engine that turns a shaft. The shaft on a helicopter is attached to its rotary blades.

Index